Daniel
Faithful Captive

LOU HEATH • ILLUSTRATED BY **J. WILLIAM MYERS, JR.**

BROADMAN PRESS
Nashville, Tennessee

4242-31
ISBN: 0-8054-4231-6

Dewey Decimal Classification: J221.92
Subject heading: DANIEL, PROPHET
Printed in the United States of America

Contents

A Prince Becomes a Slave

Daniel and his friends were tired. They had been traveling for about two months. Nebuchadnezzar, king of Babylon, had brought soldiers to Jerusalem and captured the city. He took many of the people of Jerusalem back to Babylon with him, including Daniel and three of his friends.

It was a long, hard journey. But at last they came to the great city. The young boys followed the soldiers through the huge Ishtar Gate.

"Look how deep the moat is! See how thick and high the walls are!" the boys may have whispered to one another.

Daniel and his friends were between the two great walls surrounding the city. Beautiful gardens and fruit trees were everywhere.

King Nebuchadnezzar lived in a palace just inside the second wall. He sent for his chief servant. "Ashpenaz, choose some of the young men from Jerusalem who you think will be good students and helpers to me."

Among those chosen by Ashpenaz were the sons of royalty: Daniel and his friends. Ashpenaz gave these new names to the young friends:

Daniel was called Belteshazzar;
Hananiah was named Shadrach;
Mishael was named Meshach;
Azariah was called Abednego.

Ashpenaz told the four friends about the king's plan: "For three years you will study. You will live in the palace and eat the food prepared in the king's own kitchen."

Rich foods and wine were brought to Daniel and his friends. Daniel knew that this food was not what the Jewish law said should be eaten. He talked to Ashpenaz. "Please give us vegetables to eat and water to drink."

Ashpenaz liked the boys from Jerusalem. He wanted to help them, but he was afraid. "Oh, no!" Ashpenaz replied. "If you do not eat what the king orders, you will not be healthy. I will be killed for not obeying the king."

Ashpenaz assigned Melzar to take care of the four boys. Daniel talked to Melzar. "Would you bring us vegetables and water for just ten days instead of the food from the king's table? At the end of that time you can decide whether we are healthy."

The servant thought of how well Daniel and his friends did their work. "We will try your plan and see what happens," he said.

After ten days, Daniel, Shadrach, Meshach, and Abednego looked healthier than those who were eating foods sent by the king. So for the next three years the servant brought them only the foods they had asked for.

During the three years the boys worked hard. God helped them to be good students. They learned to speak and read the strange language of the Babylonians. They also studied arithmetic, the stars, poetry, the religion of the new land, and a kind of picture writing called cuneiform writing. God helped them to be happy in this new land.

When the three years of school were finished, the students were called one by one to be examined by the king. The king asked many questions. He found that Daniel and his three friends were the wisest of all the students. They were also the best looking and the healthiest.

"I am very pleased with all four of you. I will ask you to help me make wise decisions," King Nebuchadnezzar said.

Daniel and his friends thanked God for helping them make good choices about food. They thanked God for helping them remember the things they had learned in school.

King Nebuchadnezzar gave the four young men important jobs in the government of Babylon.

Thinkback: What were some times when God was with Daniel? Name some times when God is with you.

How did Daniel take care of his body? How can you take care of your body?

How did God help Daniel as a student? How can God help you with schoolwork?

The Forgotten Dream

One night King Nebuchadnezzar had such a terrible dream that he woke up shaking! "I will ask the wise men of the kingdom what the dream means," he thought.

The next morning, the king could not remember the dream. He sent for the wise men. "You are wise and I need your help. I have had a terrible dream, and I want you to tell me what the dream was and what it means."

The men thought the king must be joking. "Tell us the dream and we will tell you what it means," they said.

The king became very angry. "If you do not tell me what I dreamed and what it means, you shall all be killed." Then the king said, "Tell me about my dream and I will reward you."

"If you will tell us your dream, we will tell you what it means, O King," the men said. "No man can tell what you dreamed."

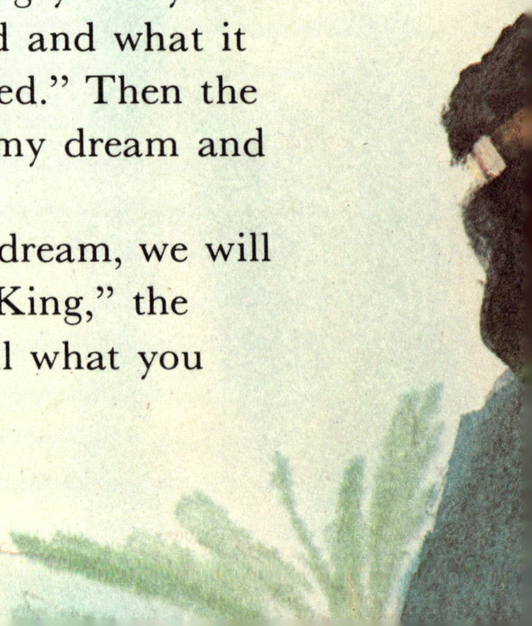

The king ordered the wise men of the land put to death. Arioch, the chief guard, went to Daniel and his friends, for they, too, were wise men.

"Why is the king so angry?" asked Daniel. Arioch explained what had happened. "Let me go to the king," Daniel suggested.

Daniel talked to the king. "Give me a little time, and I will tell you your dream and what it means."

Daniel hurried home and talked to his good friends. "Let us pray that God will tell us the king's dream," he told them.

The four friends knew that God would not let them down. Many times he had helped them. They prayed and then went to bed and went peacefully to sleep. That night God told Daniel what the dream was and what it meant.

Daniel was happy! "Thank you, God. You are a wonderful God! You know everything. You have given me a good mind, a healthy body, and now you've told me the king's dream and what it means."

Early that morning Daniel went to Arioch. "Don't kill the wise men! Take me to the king. God has told me about the dream."

King Nebuchadnezzar was pleased. "Can you tell what my dream was and what it means?" asked the king anxiously.

"There is not a wise man in all the world who could discover the dream or its meaning," Daniel told the king. "I could not tell your dream; but God, whom I love and serve, showed me your dream."

The king listened carefully as Daniel told him the entire dream. Daniel explained to the king what the dream meant. When Daniel finished, the king said, "Your God is the greatest God. Your God knows even the secrets of men."

The king gave Daniel many fine gifts. He made Daniel an important ruler in the nation. Daniel remembered that he and his friends had prayed for God to reveal the king's dream. "King Nebuchadnezzar, I would like for my friends to be my assistants."

The king granted Daniel's request. The four captives were made important rulers in Babylon.

Thinkback: What happened to King Nebuchadnezzar?

What did Daniel ask his friends to do to help him with a problem?

How was Daniel able to tell the king about the dream?

How did Daniel remember his three friends?

The Golden Idol and the Fiery Furnace

King Nebuchadnezzar looked out of a window in the palace. Babylon was a beautiful city. He had helped to make it beautiful. He looked at the ziggurat (pyramid-shaped tower) reaching high into the sky. Many of his people worshiped at the ziggurat. The king was excited. Just south of Babylon, on the Plain of Dura, he had set up a new idol. There were many idols to worship in Babylon, but this idol was unlike any other! It was ninety feet tall and nine feet wide. It was covered with layers of gold.

When the golden idol was finished, King Nebuchadnezzar looked at it. How tall it was. The king liked it. He liked the way it sparkled in the sun. Surely no idol could compare to this one! Everyone must come and see what the proud king had done.

Messengers went to every part of the kingdom. "Every prince, judge, governor, captain, treasurer, and all important men are to attend the dedication of the king's idol," they proclaimed.

Soon Babylon was filled with these important men. On the day of the dedication all the visitors gathered on the flat land of Dura before the sparkling, golden idol.

The king felt very proud as he saw the great crowd of people.

"When the music begins, everyone must bow down. This is our new god. All who do not obey will be thrown into a hot fire," the people were told. The musicians were ready. They began to play their drums, flutes, cymbals, and trumpets. The people began to fall down on their knees.

Shadrach, Meshach, and Abednego were at the dedication of the golden idol. When the music played, they remained standing. They refused to bow down and worship a false god.

Some jealous men hurried to tell the king: "The men from Jerusalem are not worshiping your beautiful golden idol. They are ignoring the orders you gave."

The king loved the young men. He could not believe they had disobeyed his orders. He sent for the three men. "Is it true that you did not obey my orders?" the king demanded.

"It is true," the brave men told the king. "The statue is not God. We worship only God."

The king was angry. "I will give you one more chance. If you disobey, I will have you thrown in a fiery furnace. Do you think your God will help you then?"

"Our God will take care of us," the three men said quietly. Shadrach, Meshach, and Abednego looked straight at the king. "O Nebuchadnezzar, we are not worried. Our God can save us from the fire, but if he doesn't we will never bow down to your golden idol."

Now the king was really furious. "Tie them up. Heat the furnace seven times hotter than usual," he shouted.

Strong guards came and tied the three men. They threw them in the roaring furnace. The king carefully watched the furnace. As he watched, his eyes grew wide in surprise. The men were walking around in the furnace as though the fire was a cool breeze blowing.

"Did you not throw three men into the furnace?" shouted the king.

The counselors answered, "Yes, O King."

"But I see four men in there," exclaimed the king. "The fourth man looks like a god! Let the men out quickly."

When Shadrach, Meshach, and Abednego came out of the furnace, the king and all the important visitors crowded around. They were amazed to see that the men were perfectly safe. They did

not even smell of smoke. Their clothing was not burned. God had taken care of them.

"These men have a god greater than my golden idol. They were willing to die rather than worship a god that was false," said the king.

King Nebuchadnezzar gave the three men more important places of service in his kingdom.

Thinkback: What was King Nebuchadnezzar's idea for another idol?

How did Daniel's friends show that they loved and trusted God?

What reason did the three friends give for not worshiping the idol?

How did King Nebuchadnezzar feel about God after this experience?

A Party with a Surprise

Some time had passed and Nebuchadnezzar was no longer the king. Belshazzar, a wicked relative, ruled in Babylon. Daniel knew that Belshazzar was not a good king. The king did not ask for God's help, for he thought his army and the thick walls around the city would keep the Persian army from entering. Besides, the city had a moat filled with water from the Euphrates River surrounding it.

Instead of praying and asking God to protect the city, Belshazzar decided to have a big party. He invited a thousand leaders in the kingdom to come to the party. As Belshazzar and his guests were eating and drinking, the king had an idea.

"Go get the gold and silver cups that we took from the Temple at Jerusalem! We will use them to drink to our gods," he told the servants.

The servants brought the cups and passed them out to the people at the party. God did not like for Belshazzar to mock him by using the special cups in this way.

Suddenly, a strange and frightening thing happened. The fingers of a man's hand began to write on the wall!

Belshazzar turned white. His knees began to shake and his legs were too weak to hold him up! Everyone grew strangely quiet in the great hall as the fingers finished writing and disappeared. The words *Mene, mene, tekel, upharsin* stayed on the wall.

"Call someone to tell us what the words mean," the king screamed. "Hurry! The one who tells me what the words mean

will have a beautiful purple robe. I will give him a fine gold chain for his neck. I will make him third ruler in all the land."

All of the people were frightened. No one could tell the meaning of the words. The queen heard what had happened. "I know a man who can tell you what the words mean," she told the frightened king. "Daniel can tell you what the words mean."

"Bring Daniel at once," Belshazzar cried.

When Daniel entered the banquet hall, the king told him of the gifts he would receive if he would tell the meaning of the words. "I do not want the gifts. You can keep them," Daniel said. "I will tell you what the words mean."

Daniel saw the gold and silver cups from the Temple on the tables. "Belshazzar, God is not pleased to see these special cups used to drink to false gods. You have not praised the one true God. God is the one who sent the fingers to write on your wall!"

Daniel looked at the words. God helped him to know what the words meant. The king would not like to hear the message. But Daniel decided to tell the evil king the truth. "Belshazzar, you have not done

what God wanted you to do. You will no longer live. Your kingdom will be divided and given to others."

King Belshazzar gave the gifts he had promised to Daniel. Then the king told all of the people, "Daniel is the third ruler in this kingdom."

That night the message from God came true. The Persian army caused the Euphrates River to change its path. When this was done, the army waded across the river and into the city. Belshazzar was killed and the city was captured by the army.

Thinkback: Who was King Belshazzar? And why was God displeased with him?

What does it mean to mock God?

Why do you think Daniel was not at the party?

Was it easy for Daniel to tell the king the truth about the message? Why? Why not?

Daniel, Faithful to the End

After Belshazzar's death, Darius became the ruler of Babylon. He divided the kingdom into 120 provinces. He chose men to be governors over the provinces. He chose three presidents to be over the governors. Daniel was chosen to be one of the presidents. This was a very important job. Daniel did his work well. King Darius was planning to make Daniel the ruler over the other presidents. Some of these men were jealous of Daniel, and they decided to spy on him.

"One day Daniel will do something wrong and when he does, we'll tell the king," they said.

Every day the men watched Daniel. Daniel tried to do the things that pleased God. He never cheated anyone; he was helpful and dependable in whatever the king asked him to do. Daniel had lived in Babylon a long time. He was about eighty years old and had been faithful to God. He spent much time in prayer. The spies finally decided on a plan that would get rid of Daniel. They went to see the king.

"Good King," they said, "pass a law that says that everyone shall pray only to you for the next thirty days. Anyone who does not obey will be thrown into a den of lions."

The jealous men knew that Daniel would continue to pray to God. The king was fooled by the jealous men. He thought they were showing how much they liked him. He signed the law, and messengers told the people.

Daniel heard about the law. He loved King Darius; however, he knew it was wrong to worship anyone but God. At morning, noon, and night, Daniel went to the window that looked toward Jerusalem. He prayed to God. The spies were watching. They went to the king and told him that Daniel had disobeyed the new law.

The king knew that he had been tricked. He loved Daniel. Daniel was his friend. Many times Daniel had helped him make wise decisions. But not even King Darius could change the law once he had signed it. The guards took Daniel and put him in the lions' den.

King Darius had never had such a bad day! A servant brought him a good supper. "I cannot eat when my friend Daniel is in the lions' den," the king said sadly.

All night the king walked up and down. He could not sleep. When morning came, he hurried to the lions' den. "Daniel! Daniel!" he called. "Please answer me. Are you there? Did your God take care of you?"

The king could hardly believe his ears! In a strong voice Daniel answered, "O King, God shut the lions' mouths. My God has kept me safe."

The king wrote a new law. It said: "Let everyone know that Daniel's God is the true God. His God can do mighty wonders. We will worhip Daniel's God."

So Daniel was famous and greatly helped King Darius. After Darius, when Cyrus became the king, Daniel also helped. God loved Daniel and gave him many blessings.

Thinkback: Why were some people jealous of Daniel?

Did Daniel deserve the honors given to him by the different kings? Why?

How do you know that Daniel loved God more than anything else in the world?

Reflections

Daniel decided some things he would or would not do while he was a young boy. He made his decisions by what he thought God would want him to do. Can you think of some things you can decide to do that will help you as you grow to be the kind of person God would want you to be? Could you be like Daniel and . . .

- Say no to the things that are not good for your body?
- Practice telling the truth?
- Worship only God?
- Pray each day that God will help you do your best work wherever you are?

EUPHRATES
RIVER
BABYLON
PLAIN OF DURA
RAMAH
BETHEL
JERUSALEM
BETHLEHEM
HEBRON
MOAB
SOME OLD TESTAMENT
PLACES